THE FRAGRANT PAST
Perfumes of Cleopatra and Julius Caesar

GIUSEPPE DONATO - MONIQUE SEEFRIED

Emory University Museum of Art and Archaeology
Atlanta

April 5 - June 25, 1989

CARL A. RUDISILL LIBRARY
LENOIR-RHYNE COLLEGE

ISTITUTO POLIGRAFICO E ZECCA DELLO STATO

Table of Contents

Foreword . . . . Pag.   5

Acknowledgments . . . . »   7

Introduction . . . . »   9

Experimental Archaeology . . . . »   13

Cleopatra's Cosmetic Workshop . . . . »   19

Ancient Ingredients . . . . »   23

Perfume and Spice Routes in the Ancient World . . . . . »   47

Perfume in Roman Daily Life . . . . »   51

Selected Bibliography . . . . »   61

The catalogue for the exhibition was made possible through the
generosity of the Istituto Poligrafico e Zecca dello Stato
(the Italian State Printing House and Mint)

Foreword

The study of ancient perfume is a rewarding task, especially when the natural result is a recreation of the actual fragrances worn two thousand years ago. Like other projects that have been undertaken in the last two years at the Emory University Museum, this exhibition is the result of international collaboration. Prof. Giuseppe Donato, Director Emeritus of the Laboratory of Experimental Archaeology at the National Research Council of Italy, first made the results of his pioneering research known in an earlier exhibition, Aphrodite's Scents, which included some of the findings in this catalogue, but he has since then arrived at yet more discoveries and conclusions, which we are pleased to communicate for the first time in print.

Dr. Monique Seefried, Curator of Near Eastern Art at the Emory University Museum, has combined Prof. Donato's research with her own study of the use of ancient perfume in Roman daily life, and contributed a thoughtful and provocative essay to the catalogue, as well as ably curating the exhibition in Atlanta. Judy Raggi Moore provided invaluable assistance in translating some of Prof. Donato's text. Lori S. Iliff capably arranged the transportation of these precious unguents and related objects of the early imperial period. Patrick Dowdey designed and installed the exhibition together with Dr. Seefried, Robert Evans oversaw the graphic design for the project, and other members of the staff saw the project to completion, including Catherine Howett, Dr.

Pamela Russell, Janece Shaffer, Jacqueline Van Eyl, and Rachanice Tate.

I wish to acknowledge the generosity of the Trustees and Directors of the Corning Museum of Glass, the Oriental Institute of the University of Chicago, and the University Museum of the University of Pennsylvania for lending works to the exhibition, as well as Mr. and Mrs. Lawrence A. Fleischman.

Finally, it is my pleasure to convey our profound gratitude to the sponsors of the exhibition. Mr. Solomon Sutker graciously made possible the preparation for and installation of the exhibit through the Sara Smith Sutker and Solomon Sutker Fund. *Dr. Giuseppe Di Milia of the Italian Trade Commission was most helpful in the initial planning stages of the exhibition. The Istituto Poligrafico e Zecca dello Stato (the Italian State Printing House and Mint), through its president, the Honorable Giuseppe La Loggia, its director, Dr. Alfredo Maggi, and its Overseas Section Chief, Dr. Luigi De Mitri, very generously agreed to assume the costs for producing the catalogue. It is our hope that this exhibition will not only edify and delight its visitors, but also contribute to their fuller sense of the achievements and sophistication of the classical world.*

MAXWELL L. ANDERSON
Atlanta

Acknowledgments

Because of my long-standing interest in the history of glass and glass vessels, it has been a natural extension of my work to turn to the history of the perfume contained in those glass bottles. My curatorial association with the Emory University Museum of Art and Archaeology goes back to 1982 when I began the re-organization of the collections. After the renovation of the museum in 1985 and the appointment of a new director, Maxwell L. Anderson, in 1987, I was given the opportunity to curate an innovative exhibition which documents the role perfume played in Roman times.

It has been a very rewarding experience to collaborate with Prof. Giuseppe Donato who has contributed so much to the success of this exhibition. Prof. Donato is a true pioneer in the field of experimental archaeology. Furthermore, I thank Dr. Anderson and the museum staff for their support. In particular, I am grateful to Lori Iliff, Coordinator of Operations/Registrar for arranging the loan of objects and to Dr. Pamela Russell, Coordinator of Educational Programs for reviewing the manuscript. Dr. Patricia Marzilli contributed many invaluable comments on the chapter about ancient ingredients.

MONIQUE SEEFRIED, Ph.D.
Curator of Near Eastern Art
Emory University Museum of Art and Archaeology

Introduction

The perfumes in Rome were the culmination of a long tradition of perfume-making in the ancient world. The origins of perfumery are lost in the mists of antiquity but there is no doubt that the history of perfume parallels the history of mankind. Sweet smells and essences of flowers were part of all primitive rites of worship.

The word perfume itself comes from the Latin "perfumum" meaning literally "through smoke". Perfume was used very early on in religious ceremonies, where incense served as a mediator between the worshipers and the gods, by creating ethereal roads through which prayers reached the divinities. Worshipers made offerings of perfumes to the gods to express their gratitude. Through these fragrant homages they found themselves in a kind of spiritual reverie especially conducive to devotion. Perfumes were also acknowledged to have powers of purification, fight odors brought on by disease or death, and cleanse the impure.

The sacred nature of perfumes is characteristic of all ancient civilizations. In Egypt the perfume industry was completely in the hands of priests, whose workshops were generally located in the rear of temples. Perfumes were used in religious ceremonies and in the mummification process. Egyptians, who bathed and washed frequently, were avid consumers of oils and cosmetics to protect their skin from the blistering heat of the summer sun. Perfumes were also enjoyed at banquets and large receptions where they were sprayed on the guests. Women and their servants had a core of oily unguent placed on the head that would slowly dissolve in their hair, rendering the surrounding atmosphere fragrant.

Released from their captivity in Egypt, the Hebrews brought back to their homeland the many skills they had acquired as slaves, and among these was undoubtedly the art of perfumery. Holy anointing oils played a major role in their religious practices, and aromatics were used in many rituals such as the purification of women. Esther, before being presented to Assuerus, had to be bathed in oil of myrrh and rubbed with other unguents for an entire year. As a result "she obtained grace and favor in his sight more than all the virgins" (Esther 2.12-13). Perfumes and make-up were also the means by which Judith seduced Holophernes and was able to liberate her people (Judith 10.8). The most luxurious and costly perfumes were reserved for use on couches (Proverbs 7.17). The Bible makes many mentions of perfumes but it is in the Song of Solomon that can be found the most poetic and evocative references to perfume in ancient literature, for example:

"Let him kiss me with the kiss of his mouth, for thy breasts are better than wine, smelling sweet of the best ointment (I, 1-2). While the king was at his repose, my spikenard sent forth the odor thereof. A bundle of myrrh is my beloved to me, he shall abide between my breasts. A cluster of cy-

press my love is to me, in the vineyards of En Gedi (I, 11-13). Who is she that goeth up by the desert, as a pillar of smoke of aromatical spices, of myrrh, and frankincense, and of all the powders of the perfumer? (III, 6). Spikenard and saffron, calamus and cinnamon, with all the trees of Lebanon; myrrh and aloe with the chief perfumes (IV, 14). My beloved is gone down into the garden, to the bed of aromatical spices, to feed in the gardens and to gather lilies (VI, 1)".

Solomon's love for fragrances was completely satisfied during the visit of the Queen of Sheba when she offered him a quantity of aromatic substances he had never seen before (Kings I.10.1-2). Her people, the Sabeans, controlled the trade routes and the production of frankincense, myrrh, nard, cinnamon, as well as other spices, and were the major suppliers of perfumes and aromatic ingredients in antiquity. In Mesopotamia, Sumerians and Assyrians burned an enormous quantity of incense during their religious ceremonies. Ointments were used for hair and clothing, and men even perfumed their beards. The Garden of Eden, where samples of all the fragrant plants known at this time are said to have been cultivated, was supposedly located between the Tigris and the Euphrates. Fragrances were so important in Mesopotamia that for Sardanapalos, the ultimate pleasure in life would be to die between his wives and his perfumes.

The Persians, who had been influenced in their use of perfumes by the lavish practices of the Medes, took great care in perfuming themselves. Their religious beliefs called for the burning of incense on the altar five times a day. One of the favorite pastimes at the court of the Persian Emperor was the hunt for the "golden rose", which consisted of locating a hidden incense burner made of gold by means of its fragrance. The winner received the precious object as a prize.

Emperors, satraps, and officers in the army often traveled with boxes containing their perfumes. When Darius was defeated at the Battle of Issos, Alexander discovered in the tent of his foe a casket filled with precious aromatic ingredients. Contemptuously, he had them thrown away, but after a few more years in Asia, he himself became addicted to perfumes. He had the floors of his palaces sprinkled with scents. Myrrh and other fragrant resins burned continuously in front of his throne. Alexander remained addicted to these elements of an artificial paradise until his death.

Other Mediterranean peoples, like the Phoenicians and the Carthaginians, apart from being great traders in scents and scent bottles, needed a large amount of perfumes for their religious and personal uses. The same is true of the Etruscans, whose tombs were filled with perfume bottles, hollow gold earrings made to contain scented oils, gold bracelets with small perfume containers, and bronze chests used to hold cosmetics.

But it is in the Greek world that the use of perfumes seems to have been ubiquitous, as we learn from ancient literary sources and through scenes depicted on Greek vases and sculpture. As in all ancient civilizations, perfumes were first reserved for the gods. The divine presence was always associated with sweet-smelling scents, as Hera is described in the Iliad:

"Her feet she bathes and round her body pours Soft oil of fragrances and ambrosial showers. The winds perfumed the balmy gale conveys Through heaven, through earth and all the aerial ways."
(Homer, Il. XIV. 170-174)

Perfume was one of the main attributes of Aphrodite, the goddess of beauty and love, since perfume was truly for the Greeks one of the symbols of the beauty they sought in every aspect of their lives. Aspasia, the well-known Greek courtesan who wrote two books on cosmetics and perfumes, had lengthy discussions with Socrates about the nature of beauty. In her house, there was always a perfume of rose and aloe that would, according to a contemporary, lift the visitor several steps above this earth and give him the impression of entering the Elysian Fields. By the time Greek civilization had reached its zenith, the art of making perfumes had greatly developed, and there is scarcely a writer or historian of the period who does not make a reference to their uses and sometimes their abuses. Perfume shops were one of the favorite meeting places for all classes of society, and among the many perfumes sold, one of the most popular was Susinum, that would remain fashionable throughout the Roman Empire. It is one of the seven Roman fragrances reproduced by Professor Donato and described in this catalogue. The Romans took over many Greek habits, a propensity often criticized by conservative thinkers like Juvenal:

"Over our seven hills, from that day, they come pouring, The rabble and rout of the East, Sybaris, Rhodes, Miletus, Yes, and Tarentum too, garlanded, drunken, shameless.

Dirty money it was, that first thing imported among us Foreign vice and our time broke down with overindulgence.

Riches are flabby, soft. And what does Venus care for When she is drunk? She can't tell one end of a thing from another.

Gulping big oysters down at midnight, making the unguents Foam in the unmixed wine..."
(Juvenal, Satires 6.295)

Despite this indictment of the influence of Greek sensuosity, one must acknowledge the fact that in the last century of the Roman Republic and in the first centuries of the Empire, the Mediterranean peoples had reached an extraordinary level of olfactory culture, the refinement of which we exhort you to sample.

MONIQUE SEEFRIED

Experimental Archaeology

This research effort began some fifteen years ago with the establishment within the Italian National Research Council of a Service of Archeological Subsidiary Sciences, a multi-disciplinary research center investigating archaeological questions with the help of the most sophisticated technology available. The first research opportunity that presented itself through the Service sent me to Romania. There I was invited to study the contents of a tomb of the first century A.D. located in Mangalia, by the Black Sea. Among the most important objects recovered from this sepulchre were the remains of a "beauty" case containing glass vials and bottles with traces of aromatic products. This was the start of our adventure in experimental archaeology.

The challenge that we faced was the reconstruction of a number of ancient perfumes or, more exactly, ointments. The rediscovery of ancient perfumes — one of the fundamental amenities of life in ancient society — is complicated by the limited evidence that survives. It is nonetheless a research activity which without question falls into the field of experimental archaeology.

The reconstruction of the perfumes was carried out by familiarizing ourselves with the original methods of antiquity, and using modern techniques only for purposes of verification. This approach was rigorously observed to prevent the experimental data we obtained from producing deceptively authentic counterfeits.

A brief history of odorous substances is appropriate before explaining the techniques by which the perfumes were recreated. The term perfume is generally used for substances that produce a sensation agreeable to our sense of smell. The first perfumes were flowers, but the desire to replace the fleeting perfume of flowers with a more lasting medium led to an attempt to extract the fragrant essences contained in them. Not content with the ephemeral nature of the fragrant gifts nature provides, man has long sought to capture and preserve these sensations by extracting the active ingredients from aromatic plants. The technique of extracting perfumes from plants began with a rudimentary process of pressing which is documented in ancient inscriptions, relief sculptures and paintings. Flowers were wrapped in a cloth which was wrung until all the odorous oil or other substances had been drained from them, or the petals were mixed with fatty substances in order to yield their fragrance. Later on, the method was improved by decoction, pressing, soaking, digesting, and, finally, distilling. The last, however, primarily belongs to a period subsequent to that which concerns us in the present study.

We began our study in various museums around the world containing evidence of ancient civilizations, and noted their holdings related to perfumes and cosmetics. A thorough search through ancient literature yielded the means of identifying some of the main substances used in certain periods and places of antiquity, and particularly the fragrant substances of the classical world from the third century B.C. to the first century A.D. The primary sources in Greek and Roman texts are the *Historia Naturalis* of Pliny the Elder, the *Cosmetica* of Publius Ovidius Naso, and the *De Materia Medica* of Dioscorides. Combining the evidence of these three texts, we were able to come close to reconstructing ancient Roman procedures for concocting perfumes.

Having consulted the ancient recipes and identified the perfumes, we needed to know not only the characteristics of the fragrant substances, but also the methods of preparation, since ancient procedures of extraction clearly differed from modern ones. The process of "forgetting" modern methods and arriving at an understanding of ancient ones was long and difficult. A fantastic voyage of exploration ensued, during which we attempted, on the basis of old recipes, to reconstruct something resembling an alchemist's laboratory. We believe that during the period ranging from the 3rd century B.C. to the 1st century A.D. the final synthesis and perfection of the classical techniques of perfumery were achieved. Not until almost the 9th century A.D. were these techniques substantially improved upon, when with the flowering of Arab culture, a revolution occurred in the preparation of perfumes through the use of alcohol and the technique of distillation.

With our research concentrated on this period, it was then necessary to single out the various vegetal products mentioned in ancient sources, especially the texts of Pliny and Dioscorides. These authors satisfy two specific needs. In the field of alchemy (if the art of perfumery may be so called), we have an excellent witness in Pliny as far as the types of ingredients are concerned, but we lack completely any indication of the original quantities. By good fortune, Dioscorides is an excellent source for this quantitative information. We made considerable headway in our research by combining the two sources. Even with these guides, there remained a number of uncertainties that required resolution. We proceeded to draw up a chart of fragrant substances utilized in antiquity (cf. pp. 24-45 Active Ingredients) and to trace the complex network of trade routes in use during the classical period (cf. pp. 47-49).

In so doing we were able to establish that products reached Rome from countries as distant as China and Ceylon, as well as from Scythia and Britain, among many others. We next attempted to retrieve samples of the original substances from their respective countries of origin in order to reconstruct in the laboratory the principal ancient odiferous compounds. The search was far from easy, and our task was complicated by the fact that the names assigned to these various plants had changed frequently over the centuries.

Once the plants and their essences had been traced to specific places of origin and samples had been obtained, it was possible to proceed with the blending process, thereby obtaining a wide range of perfumes by interpreting the recipes of Dioscorides and Pliny.

Our initial attempts at recreating these fragrant substances were procedurally flawed because they were obtained by using contemporary methods and equipment. Since this contradicted the basic premises of experimental archaeology, it was deemed necessary to confirm the results by using the ancient perfumer's techniques.

The ancient perfumer's art consisted of three procedures: "enfleurage", soaking, and pressing. "Enfleurage" was used above all to make ointments, which were obtained by spreading perfumed petals over a layer of animal fat. These petals were continually replaced until complete saturation and the desired density was achieved. This method is still in use today.

Perfumed oil could also be extracted by soaking the aromatic substances in hot oil and filtering what remained.

The third method of collecting the essential substances involved pressing, either through a bag, as was the Egyptian method, or with beam or screw presses, the preferred mechanisms of the Greeks and Romans.

To this end we collected the various ingredients involved in the manufacture of the perfumes: petals, rhizomes, and caulicles (Fig. 1). They were then carefully mixed with non-acidic vegetable oil (onphacium) and allowed to soak for a long time at medium temperature (Fig. 2).

We should like to make particular mention of "onphacium" and how it was possible to obtain it, since it was basic to all the extractions. It is the oil, according to the texts mentioned earlier, produced from unripe olives, more precisely olives harvested in August (Fig. 3). We may pass over the difficulties of obtaining them and above all grinding them. Fig. 4 shows the olives in the lab, where they were allowed to soak for at least twenty-four hours. In Fig. 5 there is the first pressed batch.They will still be ground further. Fig. 6 shows the press we have and the paste obtained by grinding. Fig. 7 shows the "onphacium". The product we obtained in the laboratory is excellent. It is a slightly greasy oil, which is very dark due to the abundance of mucilage, and is practically odorless and tasteless, apart from a faint herb-like odor. It had unexpected features, especially in its lack of fats. It has so little fat that when it is spread over the skin, rubbing it a little, it is easily absorbed. The next step was filtering, followed by blending.

In accordance with the ancient recipes, the following ointments were obtained:
Rhodinum consisting of "onphacium", rose blossom, crocus, cinnabar, calamus, honey, rush, sublimated salt, alkanet, and wine.
Myrtum Laurum consisting of oil of Persia, i.e., marjoram, lily, fenugreek, myrrh, cassia, nard, rush and cinnamon, myrtle, and laurel.
Metopium consisting of bitter almonds, "onphacium", cardamon, rush, calamus, honey, myrrh, balsam, "calbono crescina," and turpentine resin.

Regale Unguentum consisting of myrobalan, costus, ammonal, cinnamon, comacus, cardamon, lavender, myrrh, trifolium, cinnamon cassia, styrax, labdanum, balsam, calamus, rush, oenanthe, pimpinellifolia, laurel, cassia, sericato, cyperus, rosewood, panace, saffron, henna, marjoram, lotus, honey, and wine.
Cyprinum consisting of cyperus, "onphacium", cardamon, calamus, rose wood, and wormwood.
Telinum consisting of fresh oil, cyperus, calamus, melilotus, fenugreek, honey, maro, and marjoram.
Susinum, the most delicate of all, consisting of lily, balsam, honey, cinnamon, saffron, and myrrh.

In accordance with Pliny's description, we kept the ointments in small stone vessels which we reproduced from original models made out of Iranian and Greek alabasters, and lapis lazuli (Fig. 8).

Having obtained the perfumes, several thoughts came to mind. For example, it seems that during the classical period sweeter compounds — that remained fresh and refined — were preferred. In addition, the perfumed substances could be ingested since the extractive element was vegetable oil. In ancient times they were added to wine and drunk.

Other important results of our work were the identification of the exact places of origin and the prices of the aromatic substances as well as their specific uses.

Finally, we know from Pliny that pretension to sophistication is an impulse not limited to the modern era. Almost all the perfumes and odorous substances were copied in antiquity; the results were much less costly but undoubtedly bore little comparison to the original fragrances.

GIUSEPPE DONATO

Fig. 1 - *Herbs, flowers, leaves, seeds before extraction of odorous substances*

Fig. 2 - *Prof. Donato immerses ingredients in the "onphacium" for a long period of time in a double boiler at a constant temperature of 30-40 degrees Celsius*

Fig. 5 - *First-pressed batch of olives*

Fig. 6 - *Press used to produce the "onphacium"*

Fig. 3 - *Olives harvested in August*

Fig. 4 - *Olives in the laboratory*

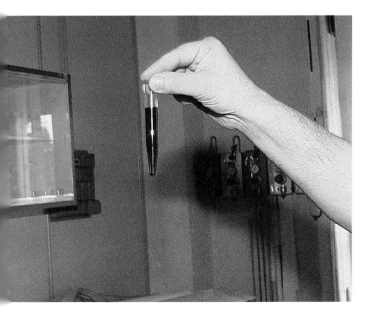

Fig. 7 - *"Onphacium," the finished product*

Fig. 8 - *The unguents are filtered and kept in small stone vessels reproduced from original models*

17

Cleopatra's Cosmetic Workshop

It was not always possible to use methods of experimental archaeology in the course of our research. In the case of Cleopatra's workshop at En Boquet, by the Dead Sea, we have had to abandon the techniques of experimental archaeology and return to a laboratory methodology based on the identification of the pollens and active ingredients found in the samples discovered in the queen's own factory. This cosmetic factory is an important archaeological discovery made by Prof. Mordechai Gichon (Fig. 9). The laboratory was found in a good state of preservation, especially the surrounding walls and the flooring.

Its structure is rather complex: it is composed of nine rooms, one of which was used as a waiting room for the clients. Its stone seats are still very well preserved. Two revolving mills for the grinding of vegetable products, two large tubs for their maceration, two kilns, and a primitive stove used for the final preparation of the ointments were found in the other rooms. All of this has been found in good condition together with the residues of the products from which the samples have been obtained. In addition, a tower had been built on the roof of one of the rooms and it was probably used to survey the nearby plantations (Fig. 10).

The factory is located in the southernmost part of the Dead Sea, approximately 30 km. south of the En Gedi oasis. The factory is thus located in the world's lowest point, at almost 400 m. below sea level, on the shore of a lake whose concentration of salts, mostly magnesium, potassium and sodium chlorides, is almost ten times higher than in any open sea. The concentration is caused by the quick evaporation of water and the erosion on the surrounding walls.

It has been ascertained that this laboratory was built during the 1st century B.C. under the reign of Herod the Great, who was particularly interested in the mineral resources and thermal springs of the area. Cleopatra was given control of the Dead Sea districts by Mark Antony (34-33 B.C.) and therefore the laboratory became her property. Cleopatra's interest in perfumes is well documented. She wrote, for example, a famous book about cosmetics. It is not known if she wrote this text before or after receiving the factory, but her work is testimony of her interest in perfumes. Although no longer extant, it was entitled *Cleopatra gynaeciarum libri* and was often quoted by Roman authors. It seems to have been a kind of recipe book that was still referred to as late as the 7th century by Paulus of Aegina.

The research carried out to isolate the organic substances in the samples collected from Cleopatra's Workshop has proven to be complex. The researchers had to discover the vegetal substances employed in the preparation of the ointments and perfumes produced in the laboratory. Pollen analyses have been made in order to identify the types of flora typical of the area. The chromatographic spectra obtained will allow comparison between the diagram of the samples collected in the laboratory and the diagrams of the standard flora singled out through the pollen analyses.

Among the wide range of plants studied, the most important was the one from which the "Balm of Judea" was extracted, intended for both medical

Fig. 9 - *Prof. Gichon and Prof. Donato
by the remains of Cleopatra's Workshop*

and cosmetic purposes. According to tradition, this shrub was brought into Israel by the Queen of Sheba who gave it to Solomon as a present.

A major ingredient used in her factory was black bituminous mud, taken from the Dead Sea, which was named Asphaltite by Pliny. Together with the mud, salts were an essential ingredient, as the following makes clear.

Below are analyses of two key ingredients used as skin treatments in the Dead Sea area. Following the mud and salt applications, the use of perfume would have been an appropriate way to cover the residual smells of these two substances.

Dead Sea mud is called Pitch of Judaea (asphalt). It is a bituminous substance extracted from petroleum through the evaporation of light hydrocarbons and the partial oxidization of the residue. The "Syrian" asphalt (from the Dead Sea) forms bright, fragile, black masses with conchoidal fractures. It smells slightly and glistens like pitch. It burns with a bright flame. Its density is 1.00-1.18. It is insoluble in water, alcohol, and acids and alkalis. It is soluble in oil of turpentine, petroleum, carbon disulphide chloroform, ether, and acetone.

Dead Sea salt is made of white and off-white crystals. It is inodorous and has a strong salty taste. Its components are magnesium, calcium, potassium, chlorides, sulphates, bromides, iodides, borates, carbonates and traces of other cations and anions. The average percentage analysis of major components are as follows: Magnesium chlorides, 32%; Potassium chlorides, 25%; Sodium chlorides, 16%; Bromine, 0.4%; Sulphates, 0.2%; Crystallized water, 26%; Insoluble residue, 0.2%.

GIUSEPPE DONATO

Fig. 10 - *Model of Cleopatra's Workshop*

Ancient Ingredients

AROMATIC REED

Genus: Vegetable

Therapeutic properties: Pliny (XXI, 72) writes "it is useful against aerophagia. It does the stomach good, stops hiccups, stimulates urination and heals the bladder".

Organoleptic properties: A balsamic, citrus fragrance, with fresh rose composition.

Cost: 15 denari per libbra.

Parts used: flower.

To Pliny it is very similar to, but less aromatic than calamus; he lists several species: Andropogon Scoenatus L., Schoenus mariscus L., etc. When rubbed it releases a rose scent (XXI, 72).

Nowadays it can be compared to verbena, balm or citronella. The aromatic reed is so called because of its similarity to the common reed. It originates in India, is reddish and knotted, and gives off a sweet fragrance. When broken, it forms numerous lamellae, which in taste are similar to cassia, with a pleasant tart sensation.

ARTEMISIA

Genus: Vegetable

Species: Artemisia Abrotanum L. (Compositae).

Active ingredients: Essential oils, resins, tannin, mucilage, insulin, abrotanin. The leaves contain vitamins A, B, B2, C.

Therapeutic properties: Antispasmodic, antipyretic (fever reducer), tonic, vermifuge (for the treatment of worms). Used for treating epilepsy. The plant is used for various ear, nose, and throat infections.

Organoleptic properties: Pleasant lemon scent.

Part used: leaves, flowering tops.

It is a bush-type herb, with a very penetrating scent. We know from Pliny that it was noted for its fresh, strong scent, and that the Sicilian variety was "very excellent". It contains elements similar to Wormwood.

BALANUS

Genus: Vegetable

It was obtained from the kernels of the *Balanites aegiptiaca*, which grows widely in Egypt and Syria. It was the most commonly used oil in the perfume industry, because it was the least viscous.

It is found among the components of most of the perfumes quoted in Pliny's and Dioscorides' texts. By pressing, oil of "Zaccana" is obtained.

BALSAM

Genus: Vegetable

Species: Commiphora opobalsamum, Balsamodendron opobalsamum (Burseraceae).

Active ingredients: Dibenzyl and benzyl cinnamic esters (75%), cinnamic and benzoic acids (12-20%), vanillin (0,08%), resin (7-8%). Weight density, 1; Acid value, 40-60. Saponification number, 133-145.

Organoleptic properties: Sweet, delicate and persistent smell; recalls vanilla.

Origin: Judaea, Syria.

Adulteration: By means of Petre Iperico, seed juice, Cyprus rose, lentisk, myrrh.

Cost: 300 denari per libbra.

Parts used: twigs, buds.

Pliny lists three species, the scents of which are superior to every other (XII, 54). The oil resin is obtained by boiling water, twigs, buds. Another product is formed by a yellowish syrup, having a citrate and rosemary-like scent; by aging the syrup becomes brown and smells like turpentine. It is also called Mecca or Judea Balsam KA-TEL, DUHNUL Balsam. It is obtained from twigs of Commiphora Opobalsamum, Burseraceae. The liquid is light brown-reddish, viscous, turbid, and has an aromatic scent. It is insoluble in water and soluble in alcohol, benzene, chloroform, acetone, glacial acetic acid, carbon disulphide, turpentine oil, ether. "The most excellent of all perfumes" — wrote Pliny — "is the Balsam which, of all the countries in the world, only India possesses". According to tradition, the Royal gardens of Jerusalem and Jericho originally had plantations of trees grown from seeds taken there by the Queen of Sheba. According to botanical studies, the plant belongs to Southern Arabia.

BITTER ALMOND

Genus: Vegetable

Species: Amygdalin communis var, amara L., (Rosenaceae).

Active ingredients: Amygdalin (1,7-3,5% glucoside), fatty oil (36-50%); in the presence of water and amygdalin decomposes to hydrocyanic acid, benzoic aldehyde, and glucose.

Therapeutic properties: The water distilled from almond owes its activity to hydrocyamic acid (0,1%), and is used internally as a sedative and antispasmodic. The powder is valuable in the preparation of cosmetics to whiten and soften the skin.

Organoleptic properties: The oil is composed of oleins, peptones, calcium, phosphorus, potassium, sulphur and magnesium.

Origin: Originally from Asia, it was introduced to Europe between the 6th and the 5th centuries B.C.

Part used: Seed.

Almonds have a tradition in the preparation of cosmetics: it is said that Cleopatra used almond milk to preserve her beauty.

CALAMUS

Genus: Vegetable

Species: Acorus Calamus L. (Araceae).

Active ingredients: Essential oil (1,5-3,5% in the Asian drug; 5% in the Japanese drug); acorin, choline, tannins.

Therapeutic properties: Stomachal and eupeptic, carminative and antispasmodic; in Indian medicine as emetic, laxative, diuretic, in intermittent fevers, sedative in some mental and nervous disorders.

Organoleptic properties: Warm, camphor-like. Good for oriental scented perfumes like amber; it mixes well with cinnamon, ylang-ylang, and costus.

Origin: India and Syria.

Cost: 11 denari per libbra.

Part used: rhizome.

It is a perennial grass that grows in marshes; it has a large horizontal rhizome covered with a brownish scale and has lanceolate leaves.

It is about one and a half meters high and produces an volatile oil contained in special "idioblasts". Every part of it is sweet and aromatic.

In ancient times several species of the same plant were called Calamus and Acorus. Pliny reports that some people name the root of Acorus oximirsine, and some of the others prefer to name it Acorus Agrarius (XII, 48).

CARDAMON

Genus: Vegetable

Species: Elettaria Cardamomum L; (Zengiberaceae).

Active species: Essential oil (3-8%) that contains cineol (5-10%), d, alpha-terpineol and its acetate, sabinene, borneol, limonene, terpinene, 1-terpene-4-ol and its formate and acetate. The fixed oil (1-2%) contains glycerides of oleic, stearic, linoleic, palmitic, caprylic and caproic acids.

Therapeutic properties: Eupeptic, carminative, indicated in chronic, non-inflammatory dyspepsia.

Fig. 11 - *Cardamon*

Fig. 12 - *Cardamon seeds*

Organoleptic properties: Spicy and camphorous odor.

Origin: Arabia, India.

Cost: 12 denari per libbra.

Part used: seeds.

There are two crops; one in February-March and the other in August-September. The fruits are harvested before being completely ripe and yellow, otherwise they open spontaneously and the seeds fall out (fig. 11).

The fruits are dried in the sun or in sheds at moderate temperature. The seed is removed from ovuls before undergoing extraction (fig. 12).

CASSIA

Genus: Vegetable

Species: Cinnamomum Cassia, Nees.

Active ingredients: See Cinnamon.

Therapeutic properties: See Cinnamon.

Organoleptic properties: Characteristic cinnamon scent.

Origin: China.

Adulteration: Storace (Pliny XII, 43).

Cost: 15-40 denari per libbra.

Parts used: bark.

It is obtained from a small evergreen bush similar to laurel.

The spice is made from the bark of the thin branches that are dried in the sun until small curled straw-like reeds are formed.

The cassia tree differs from the cinnamon because the leaves, the buds and also the roots have a scent similar to that of the bark; this is not the case with real cinnamon.

According to Pliny, Cassia is a bush and grows in the same places as cinnamon, and has a very delicate scent (XII, 43).

Columella (III, 3) tells of Arabian or aromatic Cassia.

Forbes cites *Cinnamom inermis lawsonia*.

CINNABARI-CINNABAR

Genus: Vegetable

Species: Pterocarpus Draco or Pterocarpus Santalinus L.

In Italy it is known as "dragon's blood", not to be confused with vermillion. It is so called only because of its color, it is really *Pterocarpus Santalinus L.*

The scent is characteristically heavy. The composition has an oriental note.

Pliny writes: "Cinnabari is a type of red lead, which is native or is made by burning quicksilver and sulphur. It is also known as dragon's blood." Pliny was mistaken, because Indian Cinnabari is not the "dragon's blood" mentioned above, but the resin of a tree, as Apriano rightly says in *Periplo*, and this is called "dragon's blood" in Italy.

CINNAMON

Genus: Vegetable

Species: Cinnamom Zeylanicum Nees, Cinnamomum Loureirii Nees, (Lauraceae).

Active ingredients: Essential oil (1-4%) containing cinnamic aldehyde (65-76%), linalool, eugenol (4-10%), linalyl acetate, furfural, safrole, Beta-phellandrene, methyl acetone, traces of esters.

Therapeutic properties: For internal use: stimulator of digestive functions, carminative, antispasmodic; for external use: antiseptic, astringent, mouthwash, in stomatitis and swollen gums.

Organoleptic properties: Spicy and aromatic scent.

Origin: Arabia, Ceylon, Southern China, Sudan, Ethiopia.

Cost: 15-40 denari per libbra.

Parts used: bark.

According to ancient sources, Cinnamomum and Cassia derive from the same plant from which Cinnamomum is formed (Discorides, 13 and Galenus, *Antid.*, 11).

Pliny tells of ancient tales about aromatic cinnamomum and reports that, according to some, there were two kinds of cinnamon: one white, the other and more valuable, black. He adds that the cinnamon twig has a leaf similar to that of gregan, and, when green, has no scent. Finally he says that Vespasian was the first emperor who presented cinnamon in the *Capitolium* and the Temple of Peace.

"Oleum Cinnamom'" is extracted from cinnamon. The bark is thick and rough and has a characteristic scent. The cutting of the trees takes place during the rainy season, when the bark is more easily separated from the trunk. The bark is removed from the branches as soon as they are cut to bring out the particularly fine scent. The best quality is obtained after the first cutting (Fig. 19).

COSTUS

Genus: Vegetable

Species: Saussurea lappa, (Clarke), Aplotaxis lappa D.C., (Compositae).

Active ingredients: Myrcene, p-cymol, l-linalool, sesquiterpenes, hydrocarbons, azulene, elemene, cariophyllene, cedrin.

Therapeutic properties: Very good fixing agent.

Organoleptic properties: Characteristic and lasting scent, reminiscent of iris, violet and fatty acids.

Origin: Patale Island (Indus River), Himalaya, Kashmir, Southern China.

Cost: 6 denari per libbra.

Part used: root.

It has been identified as Costus speciosus Smith (L. Domenichini, notes to Pliny's *Naturalis Historia*, Venice, 1844) or as the root of Kashmir Sessurea lappa (Forbes). It grows in India and two species are known: the black and the more valuable white. The composition is Cipro, Jasmine, Narcissus, Tuberose and fantasy. It is a herbaceous, perennial plant, that grows wild. It is harvested from September to November; the roots are dried and roasted to prevent germination.

CYPERUS

Genus: Vegetable

Species: Cyperus rotundus or Cyperus longerus L., Ligustrum vulgare (Oleaceae).

Active ingredients: Ligustrina, resin, tannin, mannitol.

Therapeutic properties: Cicatrization, detergent, in infusion or poultice.

Origin: Eastern Mediterranean, North Africa.

Cost: 5 denari per libbra.

Part used: leaves.

At times, it has been identified as Cyperus rotundus, Cyperus longerus L., and Cyperus comosus Smith because of the several names used in antiquity.

According to Pliny, Cyperus is a kind of reed (XII, 70) and the best Cyperus is the Ammoniac; then, there is the one from Rhodes and, finally, the one from Egypt which is rarely aromatic. The others should have a scent similar to that of Nard. Pliny himself says that in antiquity many could not distinguish it from "Cipiro or Gladiolus" due to the similar names.

The roots release a pleasant violet scent, which is extracted and used as lavender water. Today it is identified as Privet (Ligustrum vulgare-oleaginous family). It grows mostly wild, sometimes in the form of a bush, sometimes as a tree, often more than two meters tall, with slightly pubescent branches and oval or elliptical leaves. The flowers are in spikes.

OENANTHE

Genus: Vegetable

Species: Oenanthe pimpinellifolia L.

Dioscorides cites it as a component of Gleucinon Oinenthinon; Pliny names it when he writes of Regal Ointment (XIII, 2).

About this plant Pliny says: "It is the grape of labrusca wine... it is harvested when blossomed and has a very good scent (XIII, 61)"; ...and, afterwards he says: "the grass has parsnip leaves and many big roots..." (XII, 95).

FENUGREEK

Genus: Vegetable

Species: Trigonella foenum graecum L. (Leguminosae).

Active ingredients: Trigonelline (alkaloid), phosphorylated proteins, choline, mucilage, mannose, stachiose, lipids, lectins, proteins, albumins.

Therapeutic properties: Skin emollient, tonic, fattening; in very little quantities in oriental scents.

Organoleptic properties: sweet and spicy suggestion, recalling celery and balm of opoponax.

Part used: seed.

GALBANUM

Genus: Vegetable

Species: Ferula galbaniflua, Ferula rubricaulis, Ferula Ceraophylla (Umbrelliferae).

Active ingredients: Essential oil (4-8%; up to, in the best quality, 22%), resins (containing free umbelliferon, 0,25%), gum D.K.

Therapeutic properties: Once as balsam for chronic diseases of respiratory and uro-genital mucosa, and as a stomach remedy; now for poultices.

Organoleptic properties: Characteristic aromatic scent, bitter, warm, and pungent taste.

Origin: Syria, Asia Minor, Lebanon, Turkestan.

Adulteration: broad bean and sagapenum (XII, 56).

Cost: 5 denari per libbra.

Part used: resin exudate.
It is a gum-resin which exudes from the lower part of the plant and dries in the air.

GINGER

Genus: Vegetable

Species: Zingiber officinalis (Zingiberaceae).

Active ingredients: Essential oil (0,2-3%) with camphor scent, it contains alpha--camphene, phellandrene, zingeberene, gingerol, resins.

Therapeutic properties: Stomachal and carminative. Used as a bland revulsive, aromatic, for gargles and coloring of toothpaste.

Organoleptic properties: Lasting pleasant aromatic scent.

Origin: Southern Asia and tropical regions.

Part used: rhizome.

The plant has long leaves and large creeping rhizomes. At first it seems similar to the Iris, but on closer observation it is obvious that it belongs to a different family. It reaches a height of about 90 cm., and has yellow flowers with a spotted purple lip. The spice is contained in the root. In Asia, India and China, it has been in use since antiquity (Stobert, p. 237).

It has been variously identified with Cymbopogon acoenatus, Cymbopogon matin and Amomum Zingiber L.In the Classical era, ginger was known to come from Arabia and India.It was a small grass with white roots and spotted yellow flowers (Pliny XII, 14).

In perfumery the roots were used and prepared by mixing in wine, as for example in Rose oil.

Under the name of Aromatic Reed (Cymbopogon scoenatus), however, it is probable that it included some varieties of Cyperus in antiquity as well. Some varieties of reed were mentioned as bamboo by Pliny.

GLADIOLUS

Genus: Vegetable

Species: Gladiolus communis L. (Iridaceae).

In Pliny's time, it was believed to grow in the islands of Cyprus and Naxos, and in France.

The gladiolus from Cyprus is white and the scent is similar to that of the Nard, that from Naxos is sharper, the Phoenician one is lightly scented, while the Egyptian one has no scent whatsoever (Pliny XXI, 68, 69).

GUM - BENZOIN

Genus: Vegetable

Species: Styrax benzoin (Styracaceae).

Active ingredients: Resin (70-80%), benzoic acid 38,2%, vanillin 0,15%.

Therapeutic properties: Expectorant, antiseptic, disinfectant, and in the treatment of the skin disease scabies.

Origin: Sumatra.

Part used: This bush is native to Sumatra, and produces a balsamic resin (also called benzoin) widely used in perfumery and pharmacy and also potable liquids.

HENNA

Genus: Vegetable

Species: Lawsonia inermis L. (Litraceae).

Active ingredients: Sennotannic acid.

Therapeutic properties: Dye.

Organoleptic properties: To dye hair and nails red.

Origin: Egypt, Ascolania of Judaea, Cyprus.

Cost: 5 denari per libbra.

Part used: flowers.

Common name of Lawsonia inermis, also called alkanet, common in India, Iran, and along the African Mediterranean Coast. The paste from the powdered leaves was a cosmetic used widely in ancient times to dye hair and nails red. The scented water from flower extraction was used in the perfume industry.

It has a great importance in the beauty preparations of the Middle East. It is cultivated in European hothouses mainly because of its floral scent.

The henna is an Egyptian tree which has ziziphus leaves and coriander seeds, which are white and fragrant. These are cooked in oil and the product obtained by squeezing is called Cypro.

The most valuable kind is produced at Canopus on the Nile then followed by the produce of Ashkelon in Judaea and that of Cyprus.

Henna flowers were wonderful as perfume, and King Solomon recalls them enthusiastically in his odes by the name "Camphira".

LABDANUM

Genus: Vegetable

Species: Cistus ladaniferus L. (Cistaceae).

Active ingredients: Terpenes, benzaldehyde, acetophenone, acetic and maybe formic acid, eugenol, ledol.

Therapeutic properties: In perfumery in fine soaps; very good fixing agent.

Organoleptic properties: Sweet, herb-like, and balsamic scent, recalls grey amber, with a rich and lasting animal fragrance.

Origin: Arabia, Syria, Egypt.

Adulteration: Myrtle berries, animal excrements (XII, 37).

Cost: 4 denari per libbra.

Part used: leaf and twigs.

It is a gum resin which in the hot season exudes from the gland hairs which cover the leaves and make the plants sticky.

The leaves and the twig tops are harvested by hand in the hottest period and treated with boiling water; the blackish resin is collected from the surface.

LAUDANUM

Genus: Vegetable
Species: Cistum creticum L.
Origin: Arabia, Cyprus, Syria, Egypt.
Pliny talks extensively about this plant, and relates various hypotheses about the methods of its extraction (Pliny XII, 37): "some say that it comes from the incense tree, and is collected like rubber, by incision of the bark ...and also, it is obtained by combing the beards of goats, in which the juice is collected, as the goats nibble at the budding trunk of this tree."
When lighted, Laudanum gives forth a pleasant scent (Pliny XII, 37).

LAUREL

Genus: Vegetable
Species: Laurus nobilis L. (Laureaceae).
Active ingredients: In fruit: essence (1-9%), fatty oil (30%); in
leaf: essence (1-3%); laurel oil: laurostearin and olein, camphor and laurel essence oil.
Therapeutic properties: Sedative (for cough and whooping cough), antispasmodic (for gastralgia and vomiting); against itching.
Organoleptic properties: At the beginning, pleasant scent, like cajuput; then sweet.
Part used: leaf, tops and twigs (Fig. 13).

LILY

Genus: Vegetable
Species: Lilium Candidum (Liliaceae).
Active ingredients: Scillaren, mucilage, tannin, p-cresol, linalool.
Therapeutic properties: Emollient, expectorant.
Organoleptic properties: Subtle scent, blends with violet, ylang-ylang, jasmine.
Origin: Middle East.
Part used: bulb.
A bulbous plant, having an erect stalk. The bulb has numerous whitish flakes from which bloom basal, sessile and lanceolate leaves, which are sharp and have undulated edges (Fig. 14).

Fig. 13 - *Laurel*   Fig. 14 - *Lily*

35

LOTUS

Genus: Vegetable

Species: see Ylang-Ylang, Tuberosa, Ireos.

Pliny names several kinds of trees and herbs at various times and confuses them (XIII, 32); Celtis australis L.; Zizythus lotus, melilotus officialis L., Nymphae nelumbo L., Nymphae lotus L., etc.

In XVI, 53 he identifies it as Greek broad bean and gives a thorough description of it.

MARJORAM

Genus: Vegetable

Species: Majorana Hortensis, Origanum majorana L. (Labiatae).

Active ingredients: Essential oil (0,7 - 3,5%), tannic acid.

Therapeutic properties: stomach tonic, stimulant, diuretic; nowadays, not in widespread use, mainly associated with other aromatic herbs (thyme, mint).

Organoleptic properties: Sweet and spicy scent, recalling cardamon and nutmeg.

Part used: leaf and flowering top.

It originated in the Middle East and is strongly scented. It is thirty to sixty centimeters high and characterized by many small knots.

The Marjoram scent is similar to that of thyme, but is sweeter and strongly scented. In antiquity it was known in Cyprus and Mytilene. Marjoram oil, obtained by steeping in oil and squeezing the juice, was a component of many ancient perfumes (XIII, 2; XV, 7; Dioscorides). In Pliny's time Cizico Marjoram perfume was very fashionable. Leaves and tops produce an essence oil which has the characteristic camphor and lavender-like scent. Perfume with oriental, cologne and lavender note.

In antiquity it was called Persa or Sansuco or Amaraco. The Latins called it Amaracus, which derives from Amaraco, a royal page who tripped and fell while carrying some ointments, and from the resulting mixture created a new and most pleasant perfume (Fig. 15).

MALOBRATHRUM

Genus: Vegetable

Species: Laurus cassia L. or Laurus malabratus L. or Cinnamom tamela.

Cost: From 1 to 300 denari per libbra.

Part used: leaves.

Fig. 15 - *Marjoram*

The oil for perfume is obtained from the leaves. When put under the tongue, it makes the breath pleasant and has been used as a deodorant to scent the body and linen (XII, 59 and XXIII, 48).

"It grows in Syria and Egypt. But the best comes from India. When it is boiled in wine, its scent overcomes all others; the pure scent is by itself a noble perfume...".

MARO

Genus: Vegetable

Species: Teucrium maro L., Trifolium sipyleum L.

It grows in Libya, has small odorous leaves; the Egyptian species has bigger, less scented leaves.

MELILOT

Genus: Vegetable

Species: Melilotus Officinalis (Leguminosae).

Active ingredients: Coumarin, melilotina, glucosides, resin, flavonoids, vitamin C.

Therapeutic properties: Anti-inflammatory, anti-spasmodic, astringent diuretic, sedative. Its distilled water was used for eye-baths.

Organoleptic properties: Melilot resin oil, a sticky green liquid, with a very sweet scent.

Part used: blossomed tops.

The flowers are scented, and the plants have a pleasant aroma of honey. Basic scent of vanilla-type perfumes and of hay.

MYRRH

Genus: Vegetable

Species: Commiphora mirha L. (Burseraceae).

Active ingredients: Ether oil (containing phenols, m-cresols, terpenes, acetic, palmitic and myrrolic acid); resin (containing camphoric acid, arabmyrrol, arabresin), gum (containing pentoses and galactones).

Therapeutic properties: For internal use, in the past, in gastric atony, painful dyspepsia, diarrhea, dysentery; for external use, as an astringent and antiseptic in the treatment of inactive ulcer, angina, and mouth scurvy.

Organoleptic properties: Warm, balsamic, aromatic and mildly pungent scent.

Origin: Arabia, Ethiopia, Egypt.

Adulteration: Lentisk, gum and cucumber juice for bitter flavor.

Cost: 13-40 denari per libbra.

Part used: resin.

From the grey bark a gum-resin exudes as small yellow droplets, which become harder in the air. It is distinguished as Myrrh Eletta (pure), which has the shape of tears or irregular pieces, red-brown or reddish in color, and fluorescent and transparent; and Myrrh in Sorte, made of conglomerate dull-brown pieces mixed with several impurities. The taste is bitter and the scent is aromatic, balsamic and pleasant.

Pliny writes about it that many species are known and the most used is the one named "Statte". The trees lanced twice a year exude a gum called "Statte" which is very aromatic (XII, 35).

Some people say, erroneously, that Myrrh originates from the incense tree. According to Forbes, "dry Myrrh" was incense imported as small grains to Egypt from Southern Arabia, Lebanon, Asia Minor, Palestine, Syria, etc. (Fig. 16).

MYRTLE

Genus: Vegetable

Species: Myrtus communis L. (Myrtaceae).

Active ingredients: Beta-pinene, camphene, myrtyl acetate, aldehydes, geraniol, nerol, tannin, myrtenol.

Therapeutic properties: Aromatic, balsamic, and mildly antiseptic to the respiratory and urogenital system.

Organoleptic properites: Camphor scent.

Part used: leaf and flowering top.

Eau de cologne, fantasy, special effects, flavors (Fig. 17).

NARD

Genus: Vegetable

Species: Nardostachys jatamansi, D.

Active ingredients: Jatamansic acid.

Therapeutic properties: Antispasmodic, sedative, for treatment of hysteria, epilepsy and chorea.

Organoleptic properties: The Indian species is an herb with radical, elliptical or spatula-shaped leaves, with red flowers on the terminal spikes; the rhizomes are rich in essential oil, which has a scent similar to musk.

Fig. 16 - *Myrrh*

Fig. 17 - *Myrtle*

Origin: North India, Syria, Gaul, Crete.

Adulteration: With a herb called pseudonard.

Cost: 300 denari per libbra.

Part used: leaf and rhizome.

It is the general name given in antiquity to several aromatic plants, among which there are Nardostachys, Jatamansi, Andropogon Nardus and Celtic Valeriana. Pliny says that many things can be said about the Nard leaves. Nard is a kind of brushwood, which has a big, short, black and fragile root. It smells like Cyper. It has both spikes and leaves. One species grows along the Ganges River. It is adulterated with a herb pseudonard. The pure kind is known by its lightness and the reddish color, by the sweetness of the scent, and moreover, by the taste, since it leaves the mouth dry and has a good taste.

Also, Pliny cites Nard as the root of "Baccara" (XXI, 70-80).

Theophrastus cites Nard among the substances used as aromas.

The Nard plant which was famous in ancient times among the Egyptian, Greek and Romans, grows wild in the mountains of Nepal, Kashmir and Sikkim. It is a perennial, about 20 cm. high, with a large woody root.

OPOBALSAM

Genus: Vegetable

Species: see Balsam.

Adulteration: It was adulterated with Privet oil or honey.

Opobalsam is the juice of balsam, derived from the Greek word opos, or juice, according to Isidore (*Etymologies*, 17, 8, 14), the bark of which is lanced with iron hooks, and then exudes a extraordinary perfume from its cavities.

OPOPONAX

Genus: Vegetable

Species: Opoponax Chironium K. - Pastinaca opoponax L. (Umbrelliferae).

Active ingredients: Water-soluble gum (50-80%), alcohol-soluble gum (15-40%), essential oil (5-9%).

Therapeutic properties: Excellent fixing agent; used in oriental musk and spicy perfumes.

Organoleptic properties: Intense, balsamic, sweet and warm scent.

Part used: gum-resin.

Nowadays, it is obtained from Commiphora erytrea var, glabrescens Englar (burseraceae).It is an oily gum-resin which is collected by making some incisions on the trunk and forms a more or less regular resin material; the tear-shaped kind is the most valuable.

We know from Pliny that it grew in Syria, Africa and Macedonia; it was good for perfumes, and its juice was collected in the summer at the incision of the trunk, and in autumn at the incision of the root; its name was "Panace", from the Eraclian Panace opoponax juice was derived, commonly called "costgrass" or opoponax. The scent recalls vetiver.

ORRIS ROOT

Genus: Vegetable

Species: Iris florentina L., Iris germanica L., Iris pallida Lam. (iridaceae).

Active ingredients: Essential oil (0,1-0,2%), iridin (7-glucoside), iris camphor, myristic acid, irone, furfural, benzaldehyde.

Therapeutic properties: Violet and raspberry note.

Origin: Central and Southern Europe, Western Asia, India.

Part used: rhizome.

It is harvested in July and August, and the rhizomes are left to dry for about a week. The characteristic and valuable scent of violet develops only after aging, and the rhizomes must be stored for two or three years.

The types of iris which produce Orris Root originated in the Mediterranean area. The roots, when dried and pounded, give a powder which has a sweet scent of violet. From Pliny, who names many species, we know the scent of the iris of Corinth was very fashionable for a long time, and that the Illira iris was itself a noble scent (XII, 2). Besides, in book XXI, 83 we can read that it was used to scent wine, breath, and underarms.

The essential oil, extracted exclusively from the Florentine iris, is contained in quantities of 0, 1-0, 2% in the rhizome.

It is used in concoctions with an oriental theme.

ROSE

Genus: Vegetable

Species: Rosa centifolia L., Rosa Damascena (Rosaceae).

Active ingredients: Astringent tannic substances (17%), quercetin, essential oil that contains geraniol, citral, phenylethyl alcohol, farnesol.

Therapeutic properties: Extraordinary mounting agent in perfumes; mild astringent and antiseptic; for mouthwash and gargle use; for pomades and as corrective of scents.

Organoleptic properties: Numerous tonalities: musk, violet and sometimes fruited.

Part used: petal.

The scent is fragrant, characteristic and very refined. It is used in many valued floral concoctions.

ROSE WOOD

Genus: Vegetable

Species: Ligni Rhodii, Convulvus scoparius L. (Convulvulaceae).

Active ingredients: Linalool, aliphatic terpenes, diterpenes, methylheptenols, geraniol, nerol, d-terpineol, isovalerianic aldehyde, furfural, methyl heptyl ketone, tannin, mineral salts, glucosides.

Therapeutic properties: Choleretic, laxative.

Organoleptic properties: Characteristic sweet, mildly woody, scent.

Cost: 5 denari per libbra.

Part used: wood, roots, leaf.

It has been identified also as Convulvus Scoparius L. and wild Spartium aslalathoides. In antiquity it was identified as a small tree having flowers like those of the rose and an infinitely sweet scent (XII, 52).

It was regarded as very common, but not always scented. The Spanish species was very scented and was used to obtain an oil by steeping the plant in olive oil and, afterwards, by pressing.

In the perfume industry the root has been used after soaking in wine (XIII, 2).

SAFFRON

Genus: Vegetable

Species: Crocus sativus L. (Iridaceae).

Active ingredients: Picrocrocin, a bitter glucoside, which yields safranal, the most important part of the volatile oil in the drug (0,08%).

Therapeutic properties: At low doses, as stomachal, carminative, antispasmodic, antihysterical, and eupeptic for its aromatic property; nowadays, as dye and corrective in the Galen technique.

Organoleptic properties: Characteristic sweet, spicy, and floral scent with fatty and herb-like scent.

Origin: Silicia, Lycia, Cyrenaica.

Adulteration: If authentic, it burns the face and eyes.

1

2

Fig. 18 - *Saffron*

44

Part used: Bright red stigmas.

It is a typical crocus, with blue or purple flowers. It contains characteristic essential oils which give its aroma. It is cultivated in most Mediterranean countries, in Iran and in China. Pliny identifies it with the crocus (XXI, 81). Homer praises it along with the lotus and hyacinth. The very intense scent made ointments derived from it very pungent (XXI, 2). (Fig. 18).

STYRAX

Genus: Vegetable

Species: Liquidambar orientalis L., Liquidambar styracifula L. (Hamamelidaceae).

Active ingredients: Cinnamic acid (23%); styrol and vanillin (2%); styracine; ethylcinnamic ether; phenylpropylcinnamic ether.

Therapeutic properies: Once used as an excitant in several mixtures for antiseptic and deodorizing purposes, and as an expectorant; nowadays an antiparasitic agent (scabies, lice, etc.).

Organoleptic properties: Very aromatic.

Origin: Syria, Egypt.

Adulteration: Turpentine, resin, castor and olive oil, vegetal substance.

Cost: 8 denari per libbra.

Part used: exudated balsam.

It grew in Syria, Cyprus and Silicia, and its resin was appreciated for its sharp scent (XII, 55). Sabeans burned Styrax and produced home-made perfumes (XII, 40). It was a component of the Regal Ointment (XIII, 2). It is a balsam which exudes as a pathological product from bark and wood. It is collected from trees over four years old in the period between May and the end of Autumn, before the rainy season. It has a characteristic strong aromatic and lightly spicy scent.

The finest Styrax is collected in droplets in the hot season.

TURPENTINE

Genus: Vegetable

Species: Pinus pinea L., Pinus silvestris L., Pinus nigricans Host (Coniferae).

Active ingredients: Essential oil (28-29%), resinous acids, rosin (5-6%), bitter substance; turpentine essence, alpha-pinene and perhaps camphene.

Therapeutic properties: Seldom for internal use in chronic bronchial catarrh, in hepatic colic; for external use as a rubefacient.

Organoleptic properties: Fresh and balsamic scent.

Part used: gummy-resin.

Fig. 19 - *Cinnamon*

Perfume and Spice Routes in the Ancient World

Employed not only as condiments, spices and unguents came to be used for purposes of luxury and refinement as an integral part of life in the Roman world. This was only made possible by an incredibly complex communication network that linked many remote civilizations. The silk road and the perfume and spice routes were traveled by caravans and ships that brought the products to Rome.

"The [cave dwellers living in northeastern Africa] buy [cinnamon] from their neighbors and convey it over the wide seas in ships that are neither steered by rudders nor propelled by oars or drawn by sails, nor assisted by any device of art: in those regions only man and man's boldness stands in place of all these things they say that it is almost five years before the traders return home and that many perish on the voyage".
(Pliny, N.H. XII, 42)

This paragraph of Pliny is the missing link that enabled the reconstruction of the trade routes between 100 B.C. and A.D. 100. With this knowledge of the cinnamon route to which Pliny is referring, a complete map of the exchanges between the China Sea and the Mediterranean takes shape, forming a bridge where Eastern and Western civilizations met.

The spices had conquered Rome without meeting any opposition. At first condiments were used in abundance by every level of society (even Cato the Censor in his *De Agricoltura* recommends a recipe for cider cake enriched with anise and cumin seeds), then aromatics soon thereafter.

The market for these ingredients was at first in the hands of Greek and Semitic merchants; but after the annexation of Egypt by Octavian in 29 B.C., the Romans became able to control this profitable trade and to guarantee the uninterrupted flow of these by then indispensable substances into the capital.

According to Strabo, the Roman fleet assigned to the eastern trade in the Persian Gulf and the Indian Ocean was strengthened under Augustus. Originally consisting of about 20 ships, the fleet grew to about 100 ships as a consequence of the *Pax Romana*. The new vessels had a superior tonnage and were sent to trade for spices between India and Egypt, taking advantage of the monsoons. Even the quality of the gold and silver coins used in India improved considerably and became among the most valuable of the time. The culmination of Augustus' efforts was a trade agreement with Arab merchants, in particular the Sabeans, who controlled more of the contemporary trade routes than anyone else.

It is generally agreed that there were three spice routes (Fig. 20). One followed the silk road and meandered its way from China to the Mediterranean coast. Another was the incense route that went from the Persian Gulf to the Nile Delta and the Lebanese coast. Finally, the cinnamon road, which from Indonesia reached Rapta, a trading post not yet located with certainty, but situated on the African coast, probably facing Madagascar. From there cinnamon, various spices, and other goods, like gold, ivory, and slaves, were routed to the Horn of Africa.

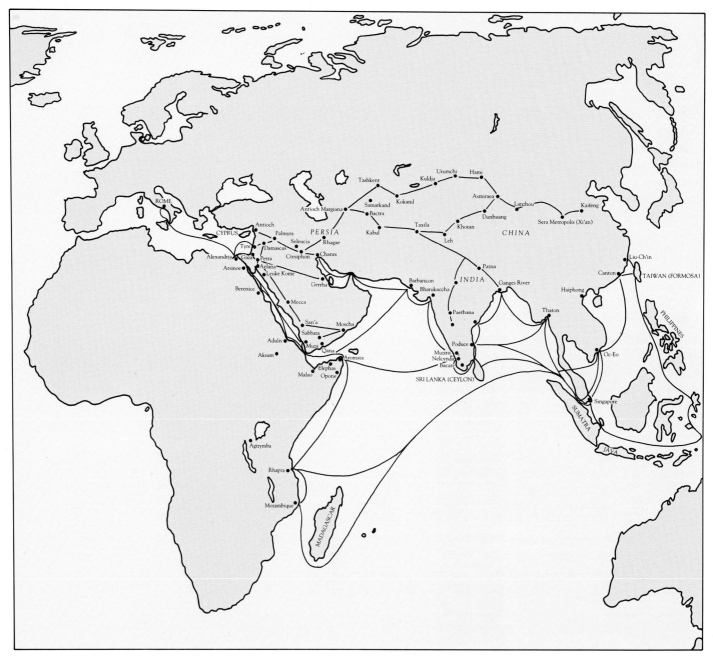

Fig. 20 - *Map of the perfume and spice routes of the ancient world*

While the Indian trade in malabathrum, sesame, curcuma (cultivated in India but native to Indonesia), cardamon, and spikenard (one of the most important scents), was secured through the sea trade, the land routes to China and Korea had become very hazardous and unreliable. To alleviate this difficulty, a maritime route to the Far East was developed with Malaysia. Malaysia became the ideal terminus for products arriving both from the north (in particular, cassia, calamus, and cinnamon), and from Indonesian islands, especially the Moluccas, which produced the best qualities of ginger, nutmeg, saffron, and cloves. The trade in Malaysia, handled by Semitic merchants, mostly Sabeans (hence the probable origin of the name Singapore, a corruption of the Latin "Sabara Emporium"), operated in two directions. One was the Singapore route, used for Indonesian trade. The other route cut the Malaysian peninsula by a series of navigable canals at approximately the current border with Thailand. The main stop on this route was Trang nel Kedah, which facilitated trade with continental Asia facing the Pacific.

Special mention must be made of the cinnamon route, the route mentioned by Pliny and traveled by the large rafts. This route was by far the most adventurous and mysterious because the Arab merchants who exploited it kept its existence under a veil of secrecy.

All the trade routes depended on a network of emporia: sites of exchange, distribution and storage. The Romans delegated the management of the *emporium* to a *mercator* who generally acted on behalf of a trading company. The Roman people were indebted to these agents for their enjoyment of many spices and scents. This web-like trade organization guaranteed that every social class could benefit from the use of ointments. They were essential to the well-being of the skin after cleansing with abrasive detergents such as beechwood ashes (lye) or finely chopped clay. These fragrant substances were also used to enhance sour wines and tasteless foods.

The value and the price of aromatic ingredients on the Roman market were determined by the difficulties encountered in supplying them as well as by the demand in the capital city. The quality of the spices also played a role and adulterations were not unknown. Pliny not only describes these adulterations, he also supplies price lists for the various spices, giving us thereby an idea of their value. The prices indicated are per Roman pound (327.45 grams) and they refer to the early imperial period. For example: cardamon, 12 denarii; cinnamon, 10 denarii; cassia, 50 denarii; costus, 5 denarii; spikenard, 100 denarii per liquid pound; pepper from 5 to 15 denarii, ginger, 8 denarii.

Cost and transportation obviously did not impede the arrival of these aromatic ingredients in Rome and their conquest of the city. Pliny complains about the use of the ointments: "Yet what is most surprising is that this indulgence has found its way even into the camp: at all events the eagles and the standards, dusty as they are, and bristling with sharp points, are anointing on holidays-and I only wish we were able to say who first introduced this custom! No doubt the fact is that our eagles were bribed by this reward to conquer the world!" (Pliny, N.H. XIII, 4).

GIUSEPPE AND ELIO DONATO

Perfume in Roman Daily Life

Early in their history, the Romans limited their use of perfume to a bunch of *verbena* hung above their doors to keep away the evil eye. Their sacrifices to the gods were also very simple: a sprig of laurel or a little corn or salt. They were then a warrior people set on enlarging their territory and not particularly interested in life's refinements.

But gradually, as their contacts with the Etruscans, Egyptians, Phoenicians, and Greeks grew, as well as with other Asian and African people, the Romans began to appreciate more and more the luxuries of life in these countries, especially perfumes, and included them in their daily life. After conquering Magna Graecia, they started adopting the manners and customs of the Greeks, not least of which was indulgence in perfumes of all kinds. In defeating Carthage in 146 B.C., the Romans became the undisputed rulers of the Mediterranean and began to import large quantitites of aromatic substances for personal use. Later, with the conquest of Arabia (A. D. 109), they would control the riches of Asia and the Far East, and a wealth of perfumes reached the city. Romans could and did from then on transport to Rome perfumery materials from every quarter of the known world.

Under the influence of Greece and the Orient, Roman sobriety was lost and those great warriors discovered with pleasure the advantages of a life where all the senses were constantly stimulated. The example was set at the top, as can be seen by the artful way in which Cleopatra seduced Julius Caesar first, then Mark Antony. She received the latter on a ship whose sails had been soaked in fragrances and whose crew was elegantly dressed and heavily perfumed. Her throne was surrounded by perfume burners and she, partly disrobed, as she had already presented herself to Caesar, was enveloped in the most inebriating perfume.

> "The barge she sat in, like a burnished throne,
> Burned on the water; the poop was beaten gold,
> Purple the sails and so perfumed that
> The winds were lovesick...." (W. Shakespeare,
> *Antony and Cleopatra*, Act II, Scene II)

The soldiers quickly adopted the tastes of their generals, and by the first century B.C., centurions went to war with their unguent caskets and perfumed their weapons. Even the eagles and the standards were anointed with precious scents before going into battle or participating in holy day parades. The victorious Roman armies took these customs back to Rome where such tastes were quickly shared by all the people.

One can well understand the need Romans could see in the use of perfumes. Rome was a very populated city, a maze of narrow streets and tall buildings (*insulae*). Although they had a very advanced sewer system, it was only connected to the public latrines and to the ground floor of buildings. The private homes had cess trenches and the tenants of the *insulae* had to empty their chamber pots into the vat placed under the well of the staircase, or by their windows, as can be attested by the many lawsuits instigated by unlucky passersby. Furthermore, many people simply used the jars put by the fullers in front of their workshops.

People of all classes lived in this unsavory atmosphere as the egalitarian instinct of the Romans had pushed them to place side-by-side the most stately dwellings and the humblest ones. In this humid and badly ventilated city, there was definitely a need to freshen the air with garlands and perfumes. Garlands made with fresh flowers or with fragrant leaves were put everywhere, on the many statues of gods and heroes erected all around the city, to decorate women's heads and crown victorious generals. To have an idea of the refinement and complexity of the fragrant garlands used on statues, in banquets, and in triumphal ceremonies, one ought to read Pliny's *Historia Naturalis*, where the major part of a book (XXI) is dedicated to garlands, giving us an idea of their importance.

The statues of gods in temples were continuously decorated with wreaths or garlands; they also had to be covered with perfumed oils while incense burners filled the air with precious fragrances. Perfume offerings were, in Roman religion, as in other ancient religions, the most appropriate way to communicate with the gods and to worship them.

In the cult of the dead, perfume also played a role, although not as important as that in Egypt. Corpses were cremated on pyres imbued with fragrances, and the ashes were subsequently mixed with aromatic substances.

Perfumes were also present in every public place. In the amphitheater, fragrant gums were burnt on altars and in lamps placed at regular intervals around the arena. The fountains were filled with scented water in order to relieve the warm and sultry atmosphere of a Roman summer, the smell of the crowd, of beasts, and of blood. In the theater, the stage was covered with saffron and the *velarium* (fabric roof) was impregnated with perfumed water that dripped on the actors and spectators. In a ceremony to commemorate Trajan, Hadrian had all the seats of the theater covered with perfume and all the guests, upon their arrival, were sprayed with a special fragrance. On another occasion, upon the death of his mother-in-law Marciana, he had a very large quantity of perfumes distributed to the people of Rome, instead of the money and foods usually distributed as *largesse*.

Perfumes were very expensive, and although cheap copies were manufactured, good quality fragrances were not affordable for everyone. Only those with well-lined purses could indulge in this luxury to the fullest extent. They purchased it in perfume shops for use in private homes and in public baths. The perfume shops, in Rome and other large cities, were one of the favorite meeting places of the idle. One went there to buy perfumes but also to chat and exchange gossip. When Amphitryon, in Plautus's comedy, is looking for Naucrates, the perfume shop is one of the first places he visits:

> "I have tramped through every street, gymnasium, store,
> Perfume shop, market, school — even the Forum;
> Gone to the doctor's, the barber's, all the shrines."
> Plautus, *Amphytryon* III, l. 1011

The perfume manufacturers (*unguentarii*) were in the same social category as doctors and apothecaries. They enjoyed enough consideration to assume honorific functions of a socio-religious character, as can be attested by funerary inscriptions. In Rome, their shops were concentrated in the Vicus Thurarius, where the best known of them, Cosmus, also had his shop. In Capua, the Italian capital of perfumery, a large area in the center of town, called Seplasia, was dedicated to the perfume industry. The *unguentarii* extracted their essences from flowers grown in Italy, but most of their raw materials came from Egypt and Asia. Pliny the Elder complains that 100 million sesterces (at his time, one sesterce was a worker's daily wage) were drained from the Empire into India, China, and Arabia, and that over half (55 million) was sent to India for spices, ointments, and gems (*N. H.* XII, 84; VI, 101). In A. D. 109, with the conquest of Arabia, supplementing the results of the Parthian campaign (A. D. 106), the riches of India and the Far East came flooding into Rome and the *unguentarii* no longer needed to worry about their supplies. They could purchase them in the Horrea Piperataria, built during the first century A. D. This was a warehouse for the reception and sale of Eastern spices and perfumes. Raw materials, as well as perfumes manufactured in Alexandria — the perfume center of the ancient world, could be found there. The well-known Roman physician Galen had his offices in the Horrea. In the Horrea Piperataria, the *unguentarii* found all they needed to produce the perfumes they manufactured. Those were divided into three categories: the solid unguents (*hedysmata*), the liquid unguents (*stygmata*), and the powdered perfumes (*diapasmata*). Of these three categories, the solid unguents were the most popular. The perfumers themselves were freedmen and they used slaves to work in their laboratories. Because perfumes were so expensive, these slaves were stripped and searched every evening before leaving.

The Romans used perfumes lavishly on themselves. Men went every day to the barber to be shaved with a rather rudimentary metal razor that left many nicks. Their sore faces were afterwards covered with hot towels and massaged with scented unguents. When Hadrian decided to grow a beard and made it fashionable, Roman men must have been elated to go without shaving. The barber also took care of their hair, often curling it or dying it before applying perfume.

In the privacy of their homes, Roman women indulged in the luxuries of their *toilette*. They bathed in bran-water or even in asses' milk, like Poppea, the wife of Nero. She was so extravagant that she had to be exiled from Rome, but, upon leaving, obtained permission to take with her some fifty donkeys to provide for her bathing needs. Perfumes were used abundantly in the bath. When one of Plautus' characters, Jackal the Pimp, sought to entice one of his clients, he describes to him wines "and perfumes! You can shower in them! Listen, we'll set up a scent shop in your steamy bathroom." (*Poenulus, or the Little Carthaginian* III, l. 700)

After the bath, the Roman woman put herself in the hands of her *ornatrices*, the slaves in charge of her *toilette*. Each had a specific function: the *tractatores* for the massage after the bath, the *unctoristes* who massaged the skin with unguents (using different ones for each part of the body), the *dropecistes* who tended to her hands and feet, the *depilaristes* to remove superfluous hair, the *calamistes* who combed, curled, and added luster to their hair, sometimes with gold dust. Blondes were a rarity in Rome and many fashionable ladies changed their naturally dark hair to a sandy or light color by washing it frequently with henna or "sapo," a bleaching substance imported from Germany. For prostitutes, dying their hair was an obligation since they were not allowed to wear it black. When the hair had dried, it was perfumed by a slave who used her mouth as the vaporizer. There was even a slave whose specific function was to perfume her mistress with her favorite fragrance. The chief *ornatrix* was in charge of a collection of pots and bottles in terracotta, marble, bronze, ivory, or glass to contain the liniments, make-up, unguents and perfumes. They were stored in a beauty case (*capsa*) that could be carried to the public baths and were generally kept in a locked cupboard in the nuptial room.

Perfumes were not only used on the body. Solid unguents were put in small containers in necklaces

Fig. 21 - *Lady at her toilet,*
Villa Farnesina,
Museo Nazionale Romano

54

and earrings. Garments were soaked in perfume, and even the soles of shoes were scented. The coats of dogs and horses were also rubbed with costly unguents. In large mansions, the walls and awnings were sometimes sprayed with perfumed oils. The inside of courtyards were washed with scented water and small trickles of saffron-imbued water ran along the floorboards of rooms in minute channels. Around the house were innumerable lamps filled with perfumed oils:

> "O battles, paired engagements, watched
>   by good-humored bed and lamp soused
> with scents from Nicero's scent-shop".
>   Martial, *Epigrams* X. 38

The cushions and pillows of the beds where Romans slept by night and reclined by day to eat, write, read, or receive visitors, were filled with dried flowers. Nero always slept on a bed of rose petals. He also bathed in rose wine. The eccentricity of the emperors reached its peak with Elagabalus, who had an entire pool filled with wine mixed with perfumes for him to bathe in with his courtiers. The wine, ennobled in such a peculiar way, was then distributed to the *plebs*.

Wine was often mixed with perfume, and this mixture was either drunk or used to anointing the heads of guests during dinners or banquets. The Romans had dinner after visiting the public baths where they frequently invited their dinner guests beforehand. Upon arriving in the house, the guests had their hands and feet washed with perfumed water. As the custom was to eat with the hands, they had to be washed between each course and slaves went with ewers from couch to couch where the guests reclined, men and women lying crosswise, two or three per couch, and administered fresh perfumed water on the diners' hands. The use of perfumes seems sometimes to have been given more importance than the meal itself:

> "Last night, at your house, you drowned us all in a
>   Beautiful perfume, but gave us no dinner.
> To be scented so well but not eat at all
>   Was it a feast or our funeral?"
>   Martial, *Epigrams*, III, 12

At certain lavish banquets, a covey of white doves, whose wings had just been impregnated with perfumes, were released for the benefit of those assembed to permeate the atmosphere. In the Domus Aurea, the emperor Nero had a very ingenious and luxurious system installed: the dining rooms were vaulted, and ivory-inlaid compartments of the ceilings revolved, scattering flower petals. They also had silver pipes which atomized unguents upon the guests (Suetonius, *Nero*, 31).

Nero had such an infatuation with perfumes that when he was invited to dinner, his hosts were required to have rose water emanating from every fountain, rose crowns on their heads and rose garlands around their necks. The dinner would end with a pink cake. It is said that at a party he gave in his villa of Baia, he spent four million sesterces for spices alone, and that for the funeral of his wife Poppea, he burned ten years' worth of Arabia's incense production. He is known to have squandered the imperial treasury on aromatic gums and perfumes. But these extravagances were not only the privilege of the imperial court. Petronius, in the *Satyricon*, discusses the end of Trimalchio's banquet as follows:

> "The panels in the ceiling began to creak--the ceiling swung open and down came a huge,round hoop. All around it were suspended golden crowns and alabaster bowls of perfumes...." Petronius, *Satyricon*, 50

Fig. 22 - Cupids acting as perfumers, fresco from House of the Vettii, Pompeii.

Fig. 23 - *Mosaic with doves, Musei Capitolini*

In less *nouveau riche* households, sawdust colored with saffron and vermillion was sprinkled on the floor. Without any doubt, at dinner parties in ancient Rome, the sense of smell was as much stimulated as the sense of taste, considering also that Roman recipes made constant use of the most fragrant spices.

If the wealthy enjoyed many perfumes in the privacy of their homes, they also used them abundantly in the public baths. The Romans were the world's most dedicated bathers. At all levels of society, they enjoyed the cleansing attributes of warm water and believed in its health-giving qualities. These public baths were as much beauty institutes in which men and women could spend many hours taking care of their bodies and minds. The baths offered them free or for little expense a sampling of all that makes life attractive. Each bath was surrounded by a portico full of shops. Inside, they could find gardens, gymnasia, rooms for massage, even libraries and museums. The baths were the most important feature of urban social life; the meeting place where Romans went every day before dinner. Until the beginning of the second century A. D., the baths were mixed; some women went to baths especially reserved for them, but the majority preferred going to those with men as well, since they enjoyed watching the sports and competitions that took place in the *Thermae*. By the reign of Hadrian (A. D. 117-138), so many scandals arose through the promiscuity of naked bathers that the Emperor passed an edict separating the sexes. From that time onwards, the hours were staggered for each sex.

These *Thermae* were really the palaces of the Roman populace, where rich and poor, emperors and artists, merchants and prostitutes, co-mingled in an atmosphere of the utmost refinement. In his description of a public bath, Seneca writes: "The walls were ablaze with precious marble, the chambers adorned with gorgeous mosaics, while the water was discharged into marble basins from silver taps." (Seneca, *Epis. Mor.* 86)

Some were huge, as in Rome, where those of Caracalla (11 hectares) or Diocletian (13 hectares) could accommodate two thousand bathers, each provided with a seat of polished marble. Upon entering, the bather undressed and handed his clothes for safekeeping to the attendants. He then proceeded to the *unctuarium*, the unguent shop, with rows of jars and vases of all kinds and sizes, each containing a perfumed oil or unguent, stacked on shelves that lined the wall. The ordinary bathers were given a supply of oil provided by the city treasury, for use as an unction. The privileged bought some costly unguents and perfumes if they had not come equipped with their personal beauty case from home, carried by their slave. For those who wanted to go wrestling, they went first to the *oleoteria* to receive an oil massage. Others went to exercise in the palaestra in order to reinforce the tonic effect of the baths on bodily health and fitness.

After exercising, one went to the *sudatoria*, a dry bath, to perspire, before entering the *caldarium*. This was the central room of the bath, a rotunda lit by the sun in the afternoon and heated by vapor. It was surrounded by small bath boxes for privacy, where vapor would come, scented with different fragrances, sensual and erotic or fresh and invigorating, depending on the activities that were to follow. In the center of the *caldarium* was a large bronze basin heated by a furnace below. One would splash the hot water on one's body with sponges impregnated with perfume, and scrape it off with a strigil. To cool off gradually, the bather went to the *tepidarium* before plunging into the cold pool of the *frigidarium*. Finally, one would return to the *unctuarium* to receive a massage of scented oils and the body was sprinkled with rose powder to stop perspiration. In order to be faithful to the Roman belief of a healthy mind in a healthy body, the bathers could enjoy the amenities of the library or the exhibition hall and stroll through the meticulously kept aromatic gardens before returning home for dinner. Despite excesses that took place in the baths and massage rooms, the *Thermae* were unquestionably a marvelous place where Romans learned to admire cleanliness, useful sports, and cultural enrichment. The Romans emerged from the *Thermae* very well scented, but some overindulged and were criticized and ridiculed by many contemporary authors.

> "Whenever you come, we think Cosmus
>   Is transmutating and cinnamon
> Flowing, diffusing from shaken glass
>   I do not wish you to pique yourself,
> Gellia, on foreign rubbish. You know,
>   I think my dog can smell sweet thus".
> Martial, *Epigrams* III. 55

Poets like Catullus and Martial invented new verbs like *fragrare, flagrare*, and *olfacere* to convey the notion of the 'sweet-smelling', but at the same time poke fun at those who are too perfumed. Pliny criticized the expense entailed by perfumes:

"Perfumes serve the purpose of the most superfluous of all forms of luxury. For pearls and jewels do nevertheless pass to the wearer's heirs and clothes last for some time, but unguents lose their scent at once and die in the very hour they are used.

Their highest recommendation is that when a woman passes by her scent may attract the attention even of persons occupied in something else, and their cost is more than 400 denarii per pound. All that money is paid for a pleasure enjoyed by someone else, for a person carrying scent does not smell it himself... I could not readily say when the use of unguents first made its way to Rome ...but good heavens! Nowadays some people actually put scent in their drinks, and it is worth the bitter flavor for their body to enjoy the lavish scent both inside and outside. "
(*N. H.* XIII, 20-25)

The last years of the Republic and the first two centuries of the Empire definitely witnessed the heyday of the use of perfume in the Roman world. Christianity took an ambiguous position towards perfumes and unguents. The word "Christos" means the anointed one, and the use of scented oils was common practice in churches, where perfumed oil lamps and scented candles burned continuously. Accepted in funerary cults, the perfumes were tolerated in daily life, but make-up and cosmetics were strongly condemned by Church fathers as they had been by pagan moralists. It would take the Middle Ages to see the use of perfumes, and for that matter the attention to personal hygiene, recede completely in Western Europe, while in Byzantium and Islam they continued to flourish and be an integral part of social customs.

MONIQUE SEEFRIED

Selected bibliography

M. Billot and F. V. Wells, *Perfumery Technology. Art. Science. Industry*, Ellis Horwood Ltd, Chichester, England 1975.

M. J. Colombani and J. R. Bourrec, *Le livre de l'amateur de parfum*, Laffont, Paris 1986.

A. Ellis, *The Essence of Beauty*, The Macmillan Company, New York 1960.

P. Faure, *Parfums et aromates de l'antiquité*, Fayard, Paris 1987.

R. J. Forbes, *Studies in Ancient Technology, III*, E. J. Brill, Leiden 1955.

K. Foster, *Scent Bottles*, The Connoisseur, London 1966.

R. Genders, *Perfume Through the Ages*, G. P. Putman and Sons, New York 1972.

H. Jefferson Loane, "Vespasian's Spice Market and Tribute in Kind," *Classical Philology* XXXIX, University of Chicago Press 1944, pp. 10-21.

W. I. Kaufman, *Perfume*, E. P. Dutton and Co. Inc., New York 1974.

E. Launert, *Parfüm und Flakons*, Verlag Calwey, Munich 1985.

Parfums de plantes, Muséum National d'Histoire Naturelle, Paris, 1987.

P. Rovesti, *Alla Ricerca dei Profumi Perduti*, di Marsilio Editore, Venice 1980.

G. Vindry, *3000 ans de parfumerie*, Musée d'Art et d'Histoire.

GRAPHICS BY OFFICINA CARTE VALORI
ISTITUTO POLIGRAFICO E ZECCA DELLO STATO
ROME, FEBRUARY 1989